DINING CARS AND DEPOTS

Patricia B. Mitchell

Published 1992 by the author at the Sims-Mitchell House Bed & Breakfast, P. O. Box 429, Chatham, VA 24531 (telephone 804-432-0595, fax 804-432-0596, e-mail foodhistory@juno.com).

Printed in the U. S. A.
ISBN 0-925117-55-2

Fourth Printing, April 1997

- A Note of Appreciation from the Author -

. . . To the staff of the Pittsylvania County (Virginia) Public Library for research assistance.

Table of Contents

Introduction

As long ago as 1550 some roads in Europe were made of wooden rails. Later on, strips of iron were fastened on the wooden rails to prevent wear and tear and to provide a smoother ride. In 1767 the first all-iron flanged rails were made in England.

Meanwhile, creative minds had been working to harness steam power. In 1774 James Watt produced an efficient steam engine, and in 1804 Richard Trevithick built the first simple steam railway locomotive.

In 1814 the Englishman George Stephenson built the Blucher, a more powerful steam locomotive which slowly pulled eight cars weighing thirty tons. In 1825 in Hoboken, New Jersey, Revolutionary War veteran John Stevens ran a small steam locomotive in the first American demonstration of steam locomotion on railroad tracks. Subsequently railroad transportation of goods and people revolutionized life in America, Europe, and around the world.

By 1873 James A. Garfield could tell an audience at Hudson College in New York, "The changes now taking place have been wrought, mainly, almost wholly, by a single mechanical contrivance, the steam locomotive. The railroad is the greatest centralizing force of modern times." [1] Trains did make life better. The powerful "iron horse" earned the respect of all and the devotion of many.

This book will explore aspects of "train mania," concentrating particularly on the food connected with railroading. The focus will be on the food served to railroad passengers, including that sold at the stations, Harvey Houses, on board, and also some food provided at special events connected with significant railroad history. From "apple-parings and paw-paws;" [2] to "bacon twirls;" [3] and "gumbo, roasted coffees and fish from the Gulf of Mexico;" [4] railroad food gave sustenance as well as a break in the tedium of travel. We will glance at today's "microwaved hot dogs and plastic-cartoned, californicated 'milk-shakes' — a five per cent milk product laced with four kinds of emulsifiers and thickeners [which] you are very well advised to shake thoroughly before opening" [5]; and elegant lobster consommé; to yesteryear's ". . . wild turkey roasted, venison steaks, and . . . partridge pie . . . [and] . . . a large jug of delicious milk . . ." [6] or the cuisine of ". . . the clever and indefatigable Mrs. Schwats, who, *it [was] said*, can kill and cook a dozen chickens in ten minutes" after receiving a signal that the train was approaching the Aiken, South Carolina station.[7] — Those tough birds certainly did not enhance the reputation of antebellum railroad travel; however, by the late 1800's as sumptuous a meal as could be had anywhere was available on the trains themselves. Railroad dining car efficiency demonstrates the fact that ". . . railroads . . . rapidly stimulated the finest engineering and innovative minds to produce thousands of original inventions and refinements." [8]

In fact, according to an October 1906 editorial by Frank Munsey, publisher of the ***Railroad Man's Magazine***:

> "The railroad, second only to religion, has been the greatest civilizing and enlightening force in the world. It has eliminated space and brought backwoods sections in touch with the polish and alertness of the cities. In conjunction with the telegraph, it has daily placed the news of the world before the farmer and the mechanic . . . . It has built up the great West . . . . [Without the railroad] we would have had no way of bringing grain and cattle from the West, no way of transporting coal from the mines and iron ore to the furnaces, or of carrying the finished product to the centers of trade. Gold and silver and copper would still largely be locked up in the recesses of the mountains." [9]

A small part of the saga of railroading can be explored by studying the food served to rail travelers. The long-ago menus, tableware, and dining car decor whisper memories, allowing us to touch the hem of history. Modern train travel creates memories for tomorrow. Let's turn back the pages of time (and our imaginary souvenir dining car menu) and look at some past "dinners in the diner."

Chapter 1

Have Candy Bar, Guitar — Will Travel Far

My first food-related train memories happen to tie into a time when railroading was no longer at its zenith — during the early 1960's. My longest trips were between Danville, Virginia, and Charlotte, North Carolina, on the Southern line. We packed fruit and sandwiches, although I seem to recall a vendor selling snacks and sandwiches in the passenger cars. I did not experience the glorious elegance and luxury of a well-appointed and staffed dining car. As a teenager, my husband traveled twice from Lynchburg, Virginia, to Kansas City, Missouri, and was aware of the fact that at Cincinnati a dining car was connected to his train, but budget considerations limited his train diet primarily to brought-along candy bars.

My early trips were made with a female cousin when we were both young teens. I mainly remember pretty country scenery, and on one special trip a friendly young male passenger with a guitar who sang us to Charlotte. Like the children in one of the ***Bobbsey Twins*** books, we found eating to be merely an entertaining way to measure the miles: a peanut butter sandwich slowly consumed might take ten miles (a far cry from the three-hour dinners on the modern AEE Express which might include lemon squash soup, *salade de saison* with hazelnut dressing vinaigrette, grilled tuna loin, with caper *beurre blanc*, roasted tenderloin of beef, wild mushrooms, bread, zucchini truffle *royale*, a cheese board, fresh fruit Napoleon, and raspberry *coulis*!).[10]

I have other train recollections, though, besides food. My maternal grandfather Charlie Jones was postmaster at Dry Fork, Virginia, and he also hung the mail pouches on a "rack" for the 4:30 a.m. and 12 noon trains to snare. The station stood just at the beginning of the upward grade as the tracks ascended White Oak Mountain, made famous by the words of the song "The Wreck of the Old 97," describing the incident involving a train which descended the other side of the mountain and accelerated too fast into Danville, a few miles south. My parents and I lived with my granddad about a quarter of a mile from the Dry Fork depot and post office, so the wanderlust sound of trains is part of my memory bank. The familiar train noises continue to soothe my psyche; my family and I live beside the Norfolk and Southern line, in easy sight of those thundering engines and their cars. The vibrations shake our glassware and rattle the windows, and the regularity of passing trains marks time almost as precisely as our grandfather clock. (Long-distance train travel and scheduling raised the nation's consciousness of punctuality and helped to bring about standardization of time.) Henry David Thoreau listened to trains within earshot of Walden Pond and wrote, "They come and go with such regularity and precision, and their whistle can be heard so far, that the farmers set their clocks by them, and thus one well-regulated institution regulates a whole country. Have not men improved somewhat in punctuality since the railroad was invented? Do they not talk and think faster in the depot than they did in the stage-office?" [11]

Besides the familiar sounds and sights of trains I enjoy now, I can think back to my Grandfather Charlie's barber shop. (He was an industrious, multi-job man!) This shop, in a room adjacent to the post office, had dark-paneled walls on which Charlie hung calendar illustrations. (He usually cut off the month pages when they were out of date and kept the upper portion.) His collection depicted full-color straining steam locomotives, so realistic-looking that they seemed to billow out sulphur scent and cinders; sleek, almost art-deco-looking diesels; many-track railroad terminals; trains curving up precarious-looking mountains; friendly cabooses. These splendid pictures were as thrilling and inspiring to me as masterpieces in the Louvre might be to a French child. They made me want to travel. They conveyed magnificent power. They stirred in me a sense of strength, an ability to press forward.

And the tales Granddaddy told! "Don't get close to the tracks when a train is going by, or the train will suck you under," he warned. No doubt my amber eyes grew wide at the thought of such a frightening possibility, yet I was somewhat (mistakenly) consoled by Charlie's story of a local fellow who had lain down between the rails as a train passed over him. That man got up unharmed, but dirty. Charlie and other "old-timers" also spoke of the "singing of the rails." – "You can hear the rails vibrate when a train is five miles away. Put your ear down near the track. Hush! Be real quiet. Now listen!"

Charlie told about fishing letters out of White Oak Creek with long sticks kept on the bank for that purpose. He had to do this fairly often because old, over-stuffed mail bags frequently burst open when tossed from the speeding trains. According to Al Emerson, postmaster after Charlie retired, "Those trains traveling at 60 mph sucked the mail [from burst mail pouches] halfway up White Oak Mountain!" (The small mail was tossed out of the mail car, but large boxes were loaded off and on the train at Dry Fork by tugging, by hand, the mail wagon over near the track. The mail wagon had four iron wheels and a long tongue for pulling.)

The Dry Fork depot did not have a dining room. It was an unpretentious gray frame structure and not very big, but across the road from the station was Bryant's store, at which passengers could buy fresh fruit, bread, candy, soft drinks, etc. Behind the store was a wooden pen in which animals were confined as they waited shipment by rail. Granddad Charlie gave $5.00 per calf to farmers who did not want to wait around until the middle of the afternoon for the train. When the train arrived to pick up the cattle (most destined to become veal in Washington, D. C. and Baltimore) Charlie was paid $6 or $7 each for the calves. Chickens and hogs were also kept in this holding pen. They, too, would find themselves on tables farther north.

Chapter 2

Flies, Rails, and Ties

The first historical reference to prepared meals being served on board train was on January 10, 1853. A caterer provided food and refreshments for passengers on two special trains which the Baltimore and Ohio Railroad ran from Baltimore to Wheeling, West Virginia, to commemorate the completion of the road (track) to that point.[12] Up until then, train travelers brought their own refreshments. As late as 1915 a journalist for the Kansas City *Star* reported retrospectively, "When everybody in the car got out their lunch baskets . . . it was an interesting sight . . . . The bouquet from those lunches hung around the car all day, and the flies wired ahead for their friends to meet them at each station." [13] (It took a good while for well-prepared railroad food to become available out West.)

On an 1830's trip to Savannah, Georgia, Fredrika Bremer sustained herself with bananas, rather than endure train depot food. In summarizing her tour she declared, "Long live the Banana!" [14]

Later on Susan Coolidge, a traveler in the West, advised packing a lunch basket for train trips. This hamper should contain, she suggested, "Albert biscuit, orange marmalade, fresh rolls, and cold roasted chicken . . . ." Most male passengers on transcontinental trips, however, scoffed at the idea of lunch baskets, pointing out that "they were always in the way and that the food was likely to spoil." [15] Ms. Coolidge, a New Yorker, also commented on depot food at various stops. "It [was] necessary to look at one's watch to tell whether it was breakfast, dinner or supper that we were eating, these meals presenting invariably the same salient features of beefsteak, fried eggs, fried potato." However, a variation appeared at the Sidney, Nebraska, station: "cubes of fried mush which diversified a breakfast of unusual excellence." [16]

Some lines did allow vendors to board trains while the trains were stopped at a station. One account tells of "mostly juveniles selling lollipops and peanuts, who roamed about the cars 'crying out their respective goods.'[17]" Another writer recalls young boys walking through the cars selling biscuits and apples. William Cullen Bryant recorded that at Fredericksburg, Virginia, "Negroes visited the cars selling cakes, fruit, and additional refreshments." Vendors also sold oranges, books, and hymnals.[18] Oscar Wilde wrote about traveling on a American train in 1882. He fussed ". . . that the boys who infest the cars and sell everything that one can eat — or should not eat — were selling editions of my poems, vilely printed on a kind of gray blotting paper, for the low price of ten cents."[19]

Mostly, though, early train travelers depended upon getting a meal at eating establishments at which their train stopped on its appointed route. Accounts of some of these dining experiences prove that train passengers were a hearty lot. Stops of only 10 or 20 minutes' duration led to many a "gulp and bolt" meal, and passengers actually suspected that some depot food was served scaldingly hot so that patrons, having paid for the meal, were unable to swallow it. Thus, it was said, the very same food could be served over and over again as each subsequent train rolled in.[20]

Other reports of lukewarm coffee, rancid butter, stale bread,[21] and biscuits so heavy they were called "sinkers," only indicate that not all depot fare was hot and tasty.

In the late 1830's popular English novelist Frederick Marryat observed that his fellow train travelers madly rushed to "refreshment stands" at which the train stopped at fifteen-mile intervals. At these antebellum "fast food emporiums" tables were laid with "pies, patties, cakes, hard-boiled eggs, ham, custards . . . ." When a bell sounded the departure of the train there was another wild stampede, this time with people grabbing up what they could carry of their food, hoping to relieve any hunger or to break the monotony of the journey "by masticating without being hungry."[22]

Nevertheless, railroads were enabling Americans to travel farther and faster than had been hitherto possible, and construction of railroads in the West was opening up new frontiers for commerce and settlement. Building a transcontinental railroad was an ambitious engineering feat accomplished by the Union Pacific and Central Pacific railroads. Tracks laid by the two construction crews met at Promontory Point, Utah on May 10, 1869. According to writer/historian Alistair Cooke, the Union Pacific work crew (mostly Irishmen) was sustained by whiskey, and the Central Pacific team (predominantly Chinese) was sustained by tea.[23]

Writer O. S. Nock states that ". . . the strategic weakness of the west coast was realised at the time of the American Civil War and in 1862, under a decree signed by President Lincoln himself construction of the Union Pacific Railroad was authorised and the work pushed forward at break-neck speed." [24] (Lincoln also ordered the creation of the first organized military railroad service, appointing D. C. McCollum — then a Colonel and later a Brigadier General — Military Director and Superintendent of railroads.)[25]

When it was suggested that Chinese workers be hired to dig tunnels and move earth and stones in laying the new tracks, railroad builder James Harvey Strobridge protested, saying that Chinese were too frail because they "ate nothing but rice." His objection was countered with the rebuttal, "Did they not build the Chinese Wall, the biggest piece of masonry in the world?" Strobridge gave in, "All right, let's hire fifty Chinese on a trial basis. If they can't cut the mustard, that's it." [26] The Chinese did indeed "cut the mustard," and more Oriental men were hired.

Construction of this railroad took millions of calories, so of course food played an important part in the mammoth undertaking. When Kansas Pacific's Irish workers ran low on bacon and beef, a twenty-one-year-old marksman named William F. Cody was hired to shoot buffalo. He guaranteed to supply all the meat the construction team could consume for $500 a month. Witnesses saw him down eleven buffalo with twelve shots. Such marksmanship kept the workers in meat and earned Cody the nickname "Buffalo Bill." [27] (Later on, Kansas Pacific train engineers willingly stopped trains to permit passengers to leave the cars and shoot at buffalo — no doubt a novel experience for Easteners!)[28]

As the line was being built, celebrations were held at certain points as they were reached by tracks. In Iowa City, for example, "a feast for all the people of Iowa City" was given, at which the first shipment of fresh oysters to reach the heart of Iowa was served, along with hot coffee and cake. This evening party lasted "till broad daylight. . . ." [29]

In Omaha, Nebraska, receptions and balls were held in conjunction with the grand project. Meals of boiled trout *à la Normande*, leg of mutton with caper sauce, quails on toast, buffalo tongue, escalloped oysters Louisiana-style, antelope with *sauce Bigarde*, "brazed" (sic) bear in port wine sauce, grouse in Madeira sauce, and teal ducks *à la royale* were prepared.[30]

Such elegant menus were a foretaste of the delicious railroad food that was to come when train officials realized, "Why should a train stop at a station for meals any more than a steamboat tie up to a wharf for the same purpose?" [31]

Chapter 3

"Railing Out Against" the UN-Civil War

Inferior and inadequate food were two factors greatly affecting the events of the American Civil War. J. B. Jones wrote in his diary on December 22, 1864, "We breakfast, dine, and sup on horrors now, and digest them all quite sullenly." [32] Railroads were largely responsible for transporting food (and other supplies), and the war actually ended when and where it did because "[t]hrough mischance, rations ordered to Amelia had gone on to Richmond. A day was lost in foraging for supplies. The following morning, at Jetersville, 7 miles southwest of Amelia, the Confederate advance force found the way blocked by Sheridan's cavalry and Griffin's infantry corps. Flanked from the Richmond-Danville Railroad, Lee turned west, toward Farmville, where rations for his men awaited him on the Southside (now Norfolk & Western) Railroad." [33] Even the nourishment from those rations was not enough to revitalize a weary, outnumbered Confederate army as the enemy closed in on them. Surrender occurred on April 9, 1865.

Throughout the conflict the "iron horse" was crucial. Both North and South depended on a rugged little locomotive known as the "eight wheeler." This famous American 4-4-0 type (four wheels on the leading truck, four driving wheels, and no trailing truck) helped to keep goods moving to the troops. (Special military uses of the railroads were developed during the war, especially by the Union forces. Armored railroad cars mounted with cannons were built. Guns and mortars were also mounted on custom-built cars.)

Both sides attempted to destroy the enemy's tracks, rolling stock, bridges, shops, roundhouses, and stations. Eventually the South's ability to wage war was weakened as the North accomplished this.[34]

Destruction of the railroad system of the South was selective, Northern troops leaving intact or rebuilding tracks which they needed. In fact, when Gen. Sherman began his Atlanta campaign in 1864, trains were running so smoothly that an average of a hundred and sixty cars a day rolled forth to resupply the Union fighting line. Retreating Confederates tore up the Western & Atlantic track as they went, but the Yankees swiftly replaced it, having been told by Sherman, "The quicker you build the railroad, the quicker you'll get something to eat." Even blowing up a tunnel near Dalton, Georgia, did not impede the Union army. "Oh, hell," one exasperated Confederate soldier exclaimed, "don't you know Sherman carries along a duplicate tunnel?" [35]

Train food during the war, like everything else, suffered. — Here, though, is an amusing story about some "dining car cuisine:"

> *"Not far from Mason and Dixon's line, a train bearing exchanged Federal prisoners on the way North stopped by the side of a train bearing Confederate prisoners to the South. The former had been provided with rations in the shape of corn pones or crusts. These pones were very distasteful to Federal prisoners who were not used to such fare, especially as they were made from 'unbolted' meal. Not infrequently this form of food proved fatal to those not used to it, but the Southern commissary department often supplied even less than this to Confederate soldiers, who, at times, ate the raw corn in the field. The 'Yanks,' therefore, were carrying some of these cornbread crusts North as souvenirs of 'Rebel' hospitality. As the trains stopped alongside of each other, the prisoners exchanged banter, and a few of the 'Yanks' threw the detested crusts into the car windows at the 'Rebs.' To the utter amazement of the former, the starving 'Rebs' devoured the crusts 'and yelled for more.'"* [36]

Chapter 4

Dinnery Finery

In 1863 the Philadelphia, Wilmington and Baltimore Railroad put two dining cars into service between Philadelphia and Baltimore. These cars were redesigned 50-foot-long coaches outfitted with an eating bar, steam box and "other fixtures usually found in a first-class restaurant." The cars remained in service for three years.[37]

In 1867 George Mortimer Pullman had introduced his "hotel car," the President, on the Great Western Railway of Canada. The hotel car was a sleeping car with a kitchen and pantries at one end, and portable dining tables. The President's menu consisted of oysters, Welsh rarebit, eggs, and broiled and cold meats for fifty cents.[38]

The first complete dining car was put into service on the Chicago and Alton Railroad in 1868. Named Delmonico, after the famous New York restaurant,[39] this swank car was operated as a first-class restaurant with lengthy menus, solicitous waiters, real china, elegant silver and glassware, and posh surroundings featuring comfortable seating, plush carpeting, and stained glass. For one dollar a gourmet-quality meal was served.[40] It was an "overnight success," for, as one earlier train passenger had complained, "Some people can not eat when they have the opportunity, and when they could eat, do not get it. Some day, no doubt, a horrible cannibalic outrage on the cars will awaken the directors to the peril of carrying starving passengers, and the luxury of the hotel-car will be instituted." [41] (In 1871 the "refreshment basket" made its appearance on the Leicester-Trent route in England. This consisted of half a chicken, ham, bread, butter, cheese, and a pint of claret or stout, all for three shillings.[42] Meanwhile, the first British restaurant car was introduced on the Leeds-London service of the Great Northern Railroad in 1879.[43] This Pullman-type car was christened the Prince of Wales, and on its open rear platform scullery boys could often be seen peeling potatoes.[44])

In 1878 the Pullman Palace dining car on the Chicago, Burlington and Quincy Railroad was advertised as:

> *". . . an eating house on wheels, an elegant restaurant within a car — just think of it — eating leisurely at a table d'hote while traveling at the rate of 35 miles an hour. Ten years ago this would have been considered an impossibility — the difference between this and lunch stations with '10 minute bolting' can be appreciated only by those who have experienced it!"* [45]

In 1879 the Palatial Hotel Cars of the Chicago and Northwestern Railway were described as:

> *". . . the finest cars ever built by the Pullman Palace Car Co. These 'Modern Hotels,' please note, are not dining cars which are run only a few miles and then switched off, but are truly what their names imply. 'Palatial Hotel Cars,' each containing a neat, cozy and clean kitchen, with china, glass and cutlery closets; a* ***Grand Saloon*** *consisting of 12 sections, with space in each for a table where meals are served. An elegant Drawing Room in which the occupants can be entirely secluded from the grand saloon if desired, conveniently arranged* ***Lavatories*** *and* ***Compartments*** *for separate use of ladies and gentlemen; supplied with every needed article to perfect an elaborate toilet. A passage way and air chamber separates the saloon from the kitchen, which effectually prevents any odors from the cooking viands from reaching the occupants of the car.*
>
> *"In the* ***Hotel Cars*** *meals are served a la carte — hence you pay for what you get and nothing more, and good meals can be got for 50 to 75 cents.*
>
> *"At night the grand saloon and drawing room are changed into a boudoir where your bed is prepared and you rest for the night as in a private bedroom.*
>
> *"It is no exaggeration to say the world does not produce the equal of these magnificent cars."* [46]

Certain railroad lines became known for specialties on their dining cars. Passengers were offered regional foods of note. For example, the Northern Pacific, which ran through Idaho, served huge baked potatoes. Bostonians on the New York, New Haven and Hartford Railroad enjoyed baked beans in miniature bean pots monogrammed with the logo and name of the railroad.[47] The Boston and Maine also dished out Boston Baked Beans; Great Northern was famous for "the Big Red Apple;" and the Southern Pacific for its "salad bowl."[48] Train passengers rolling through other western states sampled fresh trout and game, and those crossing Louisiana enjoyed Creole cuisine: "the delicacies of the South — oysters, shrimp, and strawberries in season. For breakfast there were omelets, grits, country ham, hot biscuits, and bacon twirls galore with silver pots of freshly brewed coffee."[49] French toast was a specialty of many railroad dining car chefs.[50]

In Georgia, peaches were a local delicacy. Butter "made entirely from the cream of purebred Holsteins" was served on the Twentieth Century Limited, luxury standard-bearer of the New York Central. Menus might list such exotic specialties as blue-winged teal, broiled pigeon, quail on toast, canvasback duck, and potted game, as well as roast beef, sirloin steak, cold cuts, and perhaps a dozen relishes and two dozen desserts.[51]

The printed menus themselves were artistic and colorful. Some were shaped like apples or baked potatoes. Many, of course, depicted trains. A Northern Pacific menu folder was shaped like a rounded casserole dish. Lifting the top revealed the food choices:

Oysters As You Prefer 'Em 40¢
Clam Chowder 25¢ Chicken Broth in Cup 20¢
Crab Meat au Gratin 40¢
Hot Consomme 20¢ Navy Bean Soup 25¢
Sliced Tomatoes 25¢ Head Lettuce with Egg 30¢
Finnan Haddie 60¢
Fresh Fish in Season 60¢
Boiled Ham with Spinach 50¢ Irish Stew 50¢
N. P. Special Sausage with Mashed Potato 60¢
Hamburger Steak, Creole Sauce 50¢
Roast Beef Hash 30¢
Chicken Minced in Cream with Pimentos 50¢
Great Big Baked Potato 10¢
Mince Pie 15¢ Apple Pie with American Cheese 15¢
Plum Pudding, Wine Sauce 25¢ Fruit Cake 15¢

Coffee, per Pot 10¢ Tea, per Pot 15¢
Chocolate with Whipped Cream 15¢
Individual Bottled Milk 10¢[52]

Most railroad food service operations lost money, but the lines considered superb food an excellent way to attract more passengers so that the "losing operation" dining car was not considered a problem. With opulent decor and service, wine at every meal, and such feasts as the incredible 1890 Christmas menu of the Northwestern line which offered a twelve-course dinner of forty-five different dishes[53] it is no wonder that people were eager to eat on trains.

Some "Dinnery cars," as Edith Bolling Wilson (wife of Woodrow) called them,[54] were decorated thematically. The Superchief, running between Chicago and Los Angeles in the 1930's, sported Navajo sand paintings, Indian blanket upholstery, and wood veneer. The Sunset Limited from Los Angeles to New Orleans had a lounge car resembling a French Quarter café with iron grillwork on the walls; and a dining car which evoked the feeling of a Louisiana bayou. The interior of this car was painted soft blue. The ceilings were embellished with handpainted blades of grass. On the walls hung Audubon prints of birds indigenous to Louisiana.[55]

In general, expensive furnishings such as gilt mirrors, thick carpets, rich upholstery and draperies, hand-carved paneling, and ornate light fixtures were used. Fresh flowers often graced each table.

Summer excursion trains often sported dining cars furnished with wicker because such furniture was associated with the concepts of relaxation and good health. Wicker seemed to connote "vacation." Wicker armchairs with rolled backs and arms beckoned passengers to sit down and be comfortable. The Great Rock Island Route, which was described as "the favorite Tourist Line to and from the Watering Places of the Northwest, and the Sanitary and Scenic Resorts of Colorado" ran an advertisement in *Century Magazine* (August 1890) showing a dining car brimming with spiffy-looking wicker chairs.[56]

Efficiency in the compact train car kitchen was (and is) essential. The chef and staff had to produce top-quality meals in a tiny galley. Their "restaurant" likely seated 36,[57] and the dining room was cleverly designed to maximize available space, the typical diner car length being 85 feet.[58] Even dining car dinner plates were frequently oval in shape, since in this way a narrower table could be used.[59] In the renovated, forty-seat Zurich dining car of today's AEE, weighted crystal drinking goblets lessen the chance of over-turned glasses or ". . . wine . . . dancing across the table to the rhythm of the rails."[60] The dining-car china which came to be used in the past was heavy and serviceable, and it was often especially designed and monogrammed for individual railroad lines, as was the plated flatware. These items, as well as old menus and other train memorabilia are quite collectible today. Such objects as menu holders, finger bowls, toothpick holders, silver change or tip trays are treasures. A Tabasco sauce bottle holder, china saucer and cup with matching china cover for the cup, or an elegant cut-glass syrup pitcher are rare finds today. Unique pieces of silverplated flatware exist because as many as twenty different pieces of flatware were offered in some patterns. Cheese scoops, crumb knives, oyster forks, and sugar tongs exist in addition to the more standard items. Some flatware was engraved or stamped with the railroad's initials or heralds. Covered soup tureens, fruit-cocktail bowls, bread trays, butter dishes, gravy boats, coffee servers, sugar and creamers, glass vinegar cruets, ice cream dishes, and bonbon dishes all added glamour to the white cloth-covered table.

Chapter 5

The World of the Harvey Girl

Even after the Pullman cars had brought a new level of excellence to railroad dining in the East, "western travelers were still at the mercy of the depot lunch counters." [61] Forty-one-year-old Frederick Henry Harvey, entrepreneur with a background as restaurateur, railroad mail clerk, and freight agent, arrived on the scene, convincing Charles F. Morse, superintendent of the Atchison, Topeka and Santa Fe Railroad to open a depot restaurant at the Topeka, Kansas, stop under Harvey's management. In 1876 Harvey transformed the former Topeka depot lunch counter into an appealing café. Travelers were so delighted to find good food in this mecca that one local wit reported, ". . . that the West was in danger of being settled only in Topeka" because "[t]ravellers positively declined to go further once they had eaten with Fred Harvey." [62]

The enterprising Harvey had immigrated from London, England, when he was a teenager. He was of Scottish ancestry. He arrived in America with ten dollars to his name, but soon landed a job as a bus boy in a New York restaurant. Eventually he traveled to New Orleans, and then St. Louis, where he opened a café. The Civil War redirected him on his "career track" and he became a freight agent for the Chicago, Burlington & Quincy Railroad. Harvey had 26 years combined experience running restaurants and working on railroads when he began the Harvey Houses. — It is said that ulcers caused by the poor food Harvey ate while working on the railroad was what inspired the idea for the Harvey Houses.[63]

After the amazing initial success of his Topeka depot eatery, Harvey started a restaurant and hotel for travelers in Florence, Kansas. (He paid the former chef of the acclaimed Palmer House in Chicago a phenomenal annual salary of $5000 to cook at the depot "lunch room" of this small plains town. It is said that that was more than the president of the

Florence bank received.[64]) An agreement was soon struck that Harvey would open additional facilities for the Santa Fe Railroad, with the railroad furnishing the buildings and equipment and Harvey providing food and service. He planned to establish a Harvey House every one hundred miles along the track from Topeka to Los Angeles. (At his death on February 9, 1901, he did own forty-seven restaurants, plus the franchise on thirty dining cars, fifteen resort hotels with gift shops, and the food service on the San Francisco Bay ferry system. [65])

Harvey was a stickler for quality control, often showing up for surprise inspections of his holdings. He checked windowsills for dust, and looked for chipped dishes. He was known to have yanked off tablecloths, dumping all the dishes and glassware in a broken pile when he discovered one defective plate or other piece of crockery. The Santa Fe advertised Harvey's service and food as "the standard of excellence the world over." [66]

He bought fine crystal and china, Sheffield silver, linen tablecloths and napkins from Belfast, and provided alpaca coats for improperly-clad potential patrons to wear.[67] Local food suppliers found the well-trained Harvey House chefs more than generous in paying top price for premium quality ingredients. The best was just barely good enough for Fred Harvey . . . . Harvey House chefs would pay as much as $1.50 a dozen for prairie chickens, a dime for a pound of butter, and 75¢ for a dozen quail.[68] (Harvey Houses specialized in antelope fillets, and sage-fed Mexican quail, [69] perhaps served in aspic.) A vintage claret might accompany the meal.[70] Such high standards caused happy Harvey House patrons like Alexandra Gripenberg to comment, "We were served a fine dinner made up of French foods." [71]

Just as important to the popularity of Harvey Houses as perfect mutton chops and freshly brewed coffee and tea were the wholesome waitresses whom Harvey hired. (To many lonely men out west these female "dishes" were an answer to prayer — at last a pretty, feminine face and sweet, soft voice after months or years of dusty male camaraderie!) Harvey's standards about hiring were stringent. He advertised for "young women of good character, attractive and intelligent, 18 to 30." Mrs. Harvey screened the female applicants.[72] The ladies had to sign a contract promising not to marry for a year (sometimes they "bowed to the pressures of romance" before the year was up), and also vouching for their moral character. They lived in dormitories under the strict supervision of a matron. The girls had to be in at 10 p.m. Gentlemen callers were received in the courting parlor where such "dates" were carefully chaperoned. (Even in the restaurants Fred Harvey expected decent behavior. No swearing or foul language was allowed — perhaps a novel rule to some of the rough cowpokes who wished to dine!)

The innocent, mannerly women were a startling contrast to the bar maids and floozies of the "Wild West." The waitresses wore crisp, clean, white starched aprons over long-sleeve black dresses. The only special adornment permitted was a white hair ribbon. These disciplined and nice-looking ladies were paid $17.50 per month, plus tips, and were provided their meals and room.[73]

Naturally, marriage-minded males found these waitresses most desirable, and Fred Harvey himself gave away many a Harvey House bride to grateful grooms. Supposedly 4,000 babies were christened Fred or Harvey or both in honor of the man who "'kept the West in food and wives.'" [74]

Systematic Fred Harvey developed a plan whereby his girls could satisfy train passengers' dining requirements at the station restaurants. Information was telegraphed ahead so that Harvey House waitresses had the first course on the table when the train pulled in. This was accomplished by asking whether or not diners wanted to be given a standard menu for 75¢ in the dining room, or to pay less and eat à la carte at the lunch counter. Those who had opted for the more expensive meal ate their waiting first course, simultaneously selecting their main course and beverage (served by a Drink Girl who could tell whether the diner wanted coffee, hot or iced tea, or milk by how the waitress arranged the beverage cup.) The manager usually brought the main course steaks or chops out on a huge platter and forked them over to the waitresses who then served the customers. (This was an impressive old English innkeeping custom which gave the diner a feeling of privileged treatment and plenty.) The patrons were not rushed, and menus were planned and coordinated so that customers would not get a duplicate meal on down the line in the next four days.[75] Good food, service, relaxation, and dependability made the "Meals by Fred Harvey" empire a success.

Chapter 6

Railroad Recipes and Recollections

During the Great Depression and on up through the days of my youth hobos and others lacking the cost of railroad fare rode illegally on the rails. Al Emerson, the former Dry Fork postmaster whom I mentioned earlier in this book, recalls as many as 10 to 20 men per train riding in empty box cars. It was the job of railroad detectives to catch them; then they were locked up in the county jail (of course, most were not caught).

A tree located near our house at the Dry Fork intersection had hobo markings on it (we were told) which indicated that our place was an easy mark as far as begging food was concerned. I can clearly remember scruffly, grizzly-looking train-riding "tramps" (as Mom called them), knocking on the door and asking for work, adding that they had been without food several days. Mom did not offer them any odd jobs to do, but their next plea was for a quarter or something to eat. . . . As the fellow waited on the steps, mother made up a plate of cold-cuts, left-overs, bread, and beverage and handed it out to him. The gratitude for such a meal was always quite touching.

My granddad Charlie often showed me burned-out campfires near the railroad where the hobos cooked or heated food they had somehow procured. One recipe was called Hobo Bread, which was basically biscuit dough cooked in an old tin can. If sugar, raisins, or other goodies happened to be available such ingredients might be added. Multi-ingredient, hot Hobo Stew was another specialty.

Others besides vagrants hitched rides on trains. Sometimes in logging and mining towns the company trains were a source of local transportation. In the logging town of Middle Fork, West Virginia, for example, "[p]eople rode the log trains to church and to meetings, and children sometimes hitched a ride home from school in the cab, on the cowcatcher, or 'hanging everywhere,' as one woman fondly remembers."

Eating breakfast on trains holds a special charm. Something about having "spent the night" with your vehicle makes a train breakfast seem especially meaningful. Watching the world lighten as the sun slides up the sky and the scenery slips by is an inexpressibly sweet experience. Train breakfast food descriptions often reflect the joy of waking up on the rails. Bill Rushton described food on the Southern Crescent in 1978:

> *"Breakfast in the diner, nothing could be finer than fresh bran muffins. Or the Louisiana coffee, black and thick and made with Mississippi River water all the way to Washington. There are three yellow flowers in each table's glass vase, set against the window's expanses of Mississippi wildflowers. The scrambled eggs are just runny enough to settle in the center of your plate and congeal around a large slab of ham smoked on board the train. The pot the waiter brings will hold two cups of coffee, but the morning offers no resistance to lingering over a third."* [76]

To recreate the pleasures of a train breakfast, prepare some of the following recipes:

TRANSCONTINENTAL BRAN MUFFINS

Sift together:

1 3/4 c. whole wheat flour
1/2 c. unprocessed bran
1 tbsp. baking powder
1/2 tsp. salt
1/3 c. brown sugar, packed

Beat together:

2 eggs
1 c. milk
2 tbsp. olive oil (or vegetable oil)
2 tbsp. molasses

Mix together; pour into greased muffin tins. Bake at 400° F. for 20 minutes.

Variations are many: nuts, raisins, blueberries, mashed ripe banana, candied fruit, etc. can be added to the batter.[77]

COWCATCHER SOUR CREAM BISCUITS

2 c. flour
1/2 tsp. salt
1/2 tsp. baking soda
1 tbsp. baking powder
1/2 c. sour cream

Sift flour, measure, and sift with salt, baking soda, and baking powder. Mix with cream to the consistency of a roll dough, adding sweet milk or water if too stiff. Turn onto lightly floured board. Knead lightly. Pat into sheet 1/2 inch thick. Cut with floured cutter. Place in well-oiled pan; bake in hot oven (450° F.) about 12 minutes.[78]

GEORGIA SOUTHERN SYSTEM YAM BISCUITS

1 1/2 c. plain or whole wheat flour
1 1/2 tsp. baking powder
1/4 tsp. salt
1 heaping c. cooked mashed sweet potatoes
2 tbsp. vegetable oil
Milk

Mix the dry ingredients. In a separate bowl stir together the potatoes and oil, and about a half cup of milk. Stir in the dry ingredients, adding enough milk to make a soft dough. Knead briefly, and roll out 1/2-inch thick on a lightly floured breadboard. Cut with a floured biscuit cutter. Place uncooked biscuits on a greased sheet and bake at 400° F. for 8-12 minutes, depending upon size. If the bottoms seem to be browning too quickly, turn the biscuits over using a "pancake flipper."

MISSOURI PACIFIC CORN MUFFINS

2 c. cornmeal
1 tbsp. baking powder
3/4 tsp. salt
1 tbsp. sugar
1 egg, beaten
1 1/4 c. milk
3 tbsp. bacon drippings, vegetable oil, melted butter, or margarine

Combine all ingredients. Spoon into greased muffin tins, and bake at 425° F. for 15 minutes.

Just as 19th-century traveler Susan Coolidge enjoyed orange marmalade on the rails (although she brought hers on board in a picnic hamper), you can make your own bread spread. Incidentally, an 1880 menu on the Pullman dining car "Alhambra" offered marmalade as one of the many sweet treats of a several-course dinner which went from Mock Turtle Soup through main courses such as Roast Saddle of Antelope, Boiled Beef Tongue, Roast Leg of South Down Mutton, Salmi of Duck; numerous vegetable dishes; condiments; the desserts; Roquefort and Edam Cheese and Bent's Crackers; on to Cafe Noir (black coffee).[79]

ORANGE BELT RAILROAD CO. MARMALADE

1 doz. large navel oranges
Sugar

"Cut in halves and scoop out juice. Boil the peels 2 or 3 hours in plenty of water until you can run a straw through them. Drain, and when cool enough to handle, scrape out all white, leaving only the yellow outside. Cut in straws. Weigh pulp (take from membrane) and add an equal weight of sugar. Boil pulp and straws for 2 hours and then put into glasses. It should fill 6 or 7 jelly tumblers." [80]

Train luncheon and dinner menus also have offered tempting cuisine over the decades. The train industry itself has, of course, been invaluable in its function of transporting foods across the continent. Early on, settlers in the West began to bring vast stretches of land under cultivation. Railroad posters attracted many of those people to the West by advertising. One poster in full color declared:

> *"California, The Cornucopia of the World — Room For the Millions of Immigrants/ 43,795,000 acres Government Lands Untaken/ Railroad and Private Land for a Million Farmers/ A Climate for Health & Wealth without Cyclones or Blizzards"*

This claim was illustrated with a lush, spilling-out cornucopia of citrus fruits, grapes, bananas, pineapples, pears, etc.[81] The next recipe could incorporate some of that California bounty.

UNION AND CENTRAL PACIFIC RAIL ROAD LINE
(Via Omaha or Kansas City to San Francisco)
PEAR SALAD

"This is a good mixture with which to fill canned or fresh pear halves. Also good with peaches.

* * *

8 oz. carton cottage cheese
2 tbsp. onion, chopped
2 tbsp. celery, chopped
2 tbsp. or more mayonnaise
Juice of 1/2 lemon
Salt to taste

Curry powder
Pear halves, canned or fresh
Seedless green grapes (optional)

"Combine the first six ingredients, and add a dash or two of curry powder. Drain excess juice from pear halves. Top pears with the mixture, then sprinkle with another dash of curry powder. Once in awhile I decorate filling with seedless green grapes. This mixture can be adjusted to taste!" [82]

CALIFORNIA NORTHWESTERN RAILWAY
RAISIN SAUCE

1/2 c. raisins
1 3/4 c. water or cider
1 tbsp. cornstarch
1 tsp. dry mustard
1/3 c. brown sugar, packed
1/2 tsp. salt
Few grains pepper
2 to 4 tbsp. vinegar

Add raisins to water or cider and simmer 10 minutes; combine cornstarch, mustard, brown sugar, salt and pepper.

Blend in vinegar. Stir into raisins and water; cook 3 minutes longer, stirring constantly. Serve hot with baked ham or Canadian bacon; or pour over cold sliced ham in a shallow dish and bake in a slow oven (300° F.) for 30 minutes. Makes about 2 cups.[83]

Nowadays one can hope for recognizable, tender cuts of meat on board, but this was not always so. Our already-mentioned inveterate train passenger Susan Coolidge of the last century wrote, "The chops were generally as tough as hanks of whipcord, and the knives as blunt as bricklayers' trowels." She had a suspicion that so-called "antelope" was actually leatheresque beefsteak renamed to give it the charm of novelty.[84] — Another traveler, Harvey Rice of Cleveland, noted "Here the passengers were replenished with an excellent breakfast — a chicken stew[!], as they supposed, but which, as they were afterward informed, consisted of prairie-dogs [a gregarious, large rodent]." Rice added, ". . . a new variety of chickens without feathers." Alexandra Gripenberg fared better on excursion trains. She described excellent food, saying, "We sip our oyster soup, discuss turkey and antelope steak and quail, and trifle with ice cream and cafe noir."[85] William Robertson of Scotland, however, complained of monotonous and poor-quality railroad food in the pre-Harvey House days. "[A]ll three meals . . . were almost identical, *viz.*, tea, boiled steaks, antelope chops, sweet potatoes, and boiled Indian corn, with hoe cakes and syrup *ad nauseum*."[86] Fred Harvey was indeed the "Civilizer of the West"[87] with his platters of tender meats (and waitstaffs of soft-eyed damsels).

BAKED PORK CHOPS

4 pork chops about 1 inch thick
Salt and pepper
2 tbsp. shortening
1/2 tsp. poultry seasoning
4 thick slices of onion

4 rings of green pepper
1/2 c. uncooked rice
1 1/2 to 2 cans consommé (start with 1 1/2 - if you cook longer than 1 1/2 hr. add other 1/2 can)
3/4 c. Burgundy wine

Dust pork chops with salt and pepper. Heat shortening in a heavy skillet with tight-fitting lid. Brown pork chops slowly on both sides. Sprinkle with poultry seasoning. Place onion ring inside a green pepper ring on each pork chop. Scatter rice around the chops. Pour consommé and wine over all. Cover tightly and bake in oven at 350° F. for 1 1/2 to 2 hours. Serves 4.[88]

QUAIL

4 "plump quails"
4 tbsp. butter
2 gills highly seasoned broth
2 gills port or claret
2 tsp. onion vinegar
Celery
Salt
White pepper
2 tbsp. mushroom catsup

"Cut the birds open down the back. Put the butter into the chafing dish and heat until it begins to brown. Then put in the birds, cover and cook five minutes, turn and cook five minutes longer. When nicely browned on both sides add the broth, port or claret, catsup and vinegar; season with the celery, salt and pepper, and serve." [89]

CASEY JONES'S HOT CHICKEN SALAD CASSEROLE

My mother Reba Sue Jones Beaver gave me the following recipe. (As far as I know, we are not kin to the famous John Luther "Casey" Jones who on April 30, 1900 gave his life in attempting to brake Illinois Central's Engine 382 — powering the southbound Chicago-to-New Orleans fast mail train, the "Cannonball" — before it hit two freight trains protruding from a siding in Vaughan, Mississippi.)[90]

* * *

6 chicken breasts (3 whole)
2 c. cooked rice
1 sm. onion, chopped
3/4 c. celery, chopped
1/3 c. mayonnaise
1/2 tsp. salt
1/2 c. chicken broth
2 tbsp. lemon juice
2 hard-cooked eggs, chopped
1 can cream of mushroom soup
1/4 c. pimento-stuffed olives, sliced
Potato chips, if desired

Mix all ingredients, except the potato chips. Pour everything into a baking dish. At this point you can cover and refrigerate, or cook immediately. Before baking cover with 1 c. of broken-up potato chips, if you like. Bake for 30 minutes at 350° F. Serves 4.

WELSH RAREBIT

Welsh rarebit, a traditional English dish, was on the earliest Pullman menu:

* * *

1 tbsp. butter
1 1/2 lb. fresh cheese [Cheddar]
1 tsp. dry mustard
1 c. beer

"Put butter in chafing dish; when nearly melted add cheese cut in small dice, mustard and a little cayenne pepper.

Stir all the time; add a small amount of beer to prevent burning. Keep adding beer. Serve hot on toast."[91]

CAPE COD CRANBERRY ORANGE RELISH

1 lb. bag fresh cranberries
2 ea. oranges, zest and pulp (no white parts)
1 1/2 c. light brown sugar, packed
1/4 c. Grand Marnier liqueur

"Chop all ingredients in a food chopper and mix well. Cover and refrigerate for 48 hours before serving. Use with any poultry. Yield: approximately 5 cups."[92]

SUNSET LIMITED BAKED RED SNAPPER
("A Simple Every-Day Recipe for Baking Red Snapper")

Red snapper was found not only on Gulf Coast menus but also on Northern Pacific's 1910 Christmas dinner menu. Served with Creole Sauce, the fish cost 50¢. Stuffed Quail with Bacon was 60¢, Choice Stand of Beef with Drip Gravy sold for 50¢, and Ox Tongue 35¢.[93]

* * *

1 "fine 3-pound red snapper"
2 tbsp. butter
1 large onion
3 sprigs of parsley
1 bay leaf
1 c. stale bread crumbs
1/2 tea cup of water
Salt and pepper

"Select a fine, large fish, clean and wash thoroughly. Make a dressing by taking one cup of stale bread, wet and squeezed of all water; one large onion and three sprigs of parsley. Chop the onions and parsley fine and mix with the

bread crumbs and fry in a spoonful of butter, seasoning well with salt and pepper. Stuff the fish and sew up with a soft thread. Then rub the fish thoroughly with salt and pepper and butter. Put small pieces of butter all over the fish and add a few pieces on the bottom of the baking pan. Pour in water to the depth of two inches, cover the pan and bake on the outside of the oven, about an hour and a half. When the fish is baked in the oven it partakes more of the character of roasted fish." [94]

ALASKAN GRILLED SALMON

The representative 1888 Alhambra dinner menu lists "Salmon a la Chamborg" among its extensive offerings, and the March 15, 1889 menu for the Coronado out of Chicago lists "Boiled Fresh Salmon, Shrimp Sauce/Sliced Cucumbers." Although the Alaska Railroad was not completed until 1923, the first salmon canning factory in Alaska was built in 1878. — The following recipe utilizes fresh salmon steaks.

* * *

6 salmon steaks
1 c. white or rosé wine
1/2 tsp. onion powder
1/2 tsp. dried marjoram
Dash of pepper and seasoned salt

Place the fish in a shallow Pyrex dish. Mix the remaining ingredients and pour over the salmon. Cover and refrigerate for several hours, turning over the salmon once or twice. Drain, and grill or broil.

NICKLE PLATE RAILROAD "COPPER PENNIES"

The typical recipe for "copper pennies" calls for thinly-sliced carrots. This easy dish makes "fat pennies!" — Did you every leave a penny on the railroad track for a train to flatten? They'd end up looking about the size of a fifty cent piece! My granddaddy said not to do that because it could make the train wreck!

* * *

"Scrape carrots. Cut into 1/2" rounds. Cook with small amount of water, and season with salt and summer savory. Just before serving add some sour cream." [95]

CORN FRITTERS

Corn Fritters were listed on the previously-discussed 1910 Northern Pacific menu. They accompanied a Broiled Spring Chicken for the price of 50¢.

* * *

1 c. cold sweet corn
1 egg, beaten
2 tbsp. flour
1/2 tsp. baking powder
Pepper and salt

"Make into a batter and fry by spoonfuls in butter." [96]

NARROW GAUGE NOODLE CASSEROLE

The standard distance between the rails in a track in the United States was set in the 1870's at 4 feet 8 1/2 inches. At one time there were about twenty-three different railroad gauges, ranging from 3 feet to 6 feet. As a result, cars of one railroad could not operate on many of the other railroads . . . .[97]

This simple "lite" side-dish is a pleasant change of pace from potatoes. Serve noodle casserole with barbecued chicken, roast beef, ham, etc. By the way, today's train traveler who requires a special diet can request in advance vegetarian, low-sodium, kosher, or other type of food.

* * *

12 oz. (about 4 c. dry) egg noodles, cooked
1 c. cottage cheese
1 c. plain yogurt
1/2 tsp. salt (or less)
1/8 tsp. pepper
1/3 c. onion, chopped
1 tbsp. butter or margarine

Combine the ingredients listed above, except for the butter. Spoon the mixture into a greased casserole dish, dot with butter or margarine, and cover. Bake at 350° - 375° F. for 20-30 minutes, or until plenty hot.

INTERCOLONIAL AND PRINCE EDWARD ISLAND RAILWAY OF CANADA SLICED BREAD-AND-BUTTER PICKLES

Train menus listed lots of extras: stuffed olives, green olives, chow chow, pickled onions, celery, sliced tomatoes, corn relish, gherkins, etc. — These tasty pickles would satisfy any rail traveler.

* * *

8 c. sliced cucumbers (small size)
2 c. sliced onions
1/2 c. salt

Soak 2 hours. Wash off salt, soak in ice water for 2 hours and drain. Combine:

2 c. vinegar
2 tsp. tumeric
3 c. white sugar
2 tsp. celery seed

Boil 5 minutes and pour over vegetables, let stand overnight. In morning, drain syrup and boil. Pack cucumbers in bottles — not too tight. Pour syrup over and seal.[98]

Dessert and coffee help evening roll into night on a train . . .

OLD 97 PEACH CRISP

As mentioned earlier, a major event in railroad history occurred near here, in Danville on September 27, 1903. After passing through Chatham and Dry Fork and ascending White Oak Mountain, J. A. ("Steve") Broady, engineer of the Old 97, lost control of the train on the downslope into Danville, causing a wreck immortalized in song. (That song, by the way, not only commemorated a wreck, but birthed the country music industry!)

* * *

6 or 7 large peaches
Juice of one lemon
1 c. flour, sifted
1 c. brown sugar, packed
1/2 c. butter or margarine

Wash, peel, and slice peaches. Put in a shallow 2-qt. baking dish and sprinkle with lemon juice. Mix flour and brown sugar. Cut in butter until crumbly. Put over peaches. Bake at 375° F. about 25 minutes or until peaches are done.[99]

APPLE PIE

Apple pie was served on the "Alhambra" and the "Coronado." The aforementioned March 15, 1889 menu on the Coronado offers apple pie as one of many dessert options following such delights as "Blue Points on Shell," "Sweetbreads Sauté," "Roast Spring Lamb," fresh lobster, etc. etc. This recipe will create a pleasurable dessert:

* * *

6 apples, peeled, cored, and sliced
2/3 c. sugar

1/4 tsp. nutmeg
1/2 tsp. cinnamon
1 tbsp. lemon juice
1 tbsp. butter
Unbaked double crust pastry shell

Fill pastry shell with sliced apples. Sprinkle on the next four ingredients. Dot with butter. Adjust top crust. Flute edges. Cook 1 1/4 hours at 325° F.

PULLMAN TAFFY

A good old-fashioned recipe named in honor of George Mortimer Pullman:

* * *

2 c. sugar
1/8 tsp. cream of tartar
2 tbsp. butter
1/2 c. vinegar
Few grains salt

Combine all ingredients. Boil to hard ball stage (265° - 270° F.). Cool. Pull until white and porous. Cut in 1-inch pieces.[100]

I hope you have enjoyed this culinary journey on the rails, food being one part of the mystique of those handsome steam trains and their "descendants." As Charles Klamkin wrote:

> *"The history of railroading is reflective of America's social and business history, and each timetable, annual pass, switch lock and key, lantern, or dining-car menu adds to the general knowledge of the great part the railroads played in the growth of the nation."* [101]

Notes

[1]Carolyn Stromeyer Thornton, "A Steamy Southern Affair," *Travel-Holiday*, Travel Magazine, Inc., New York, October 1986, p. 64.

[2]Lillian Foster, *Way-Side Glimpses North and South*, New York, 1860, p. 132, quoted in Eugene Alvarez, *Travel on Southern Antebellum Railroads, 1828-1860*, The University of Alabama Press, 1974, p. 197.

[3]Camilla Glenn, *The Heritage of Southern Cooking*, Workman Publishing Company, Inc., New York, 1986, pp. 20-21.

[4]Mary Clifford, "Dining Car Days," *Country Living*, May 1988, p. 172.

[5]Bill Rushton, "The Southern Crescent," *Gris-Gris*, Baton Rouge, July 24-30, 1978, p. 14.

[6]Charles Lyell, *A Second Visit to the United States of North America*, Vol. II, Harper & Bros., New York, 1849, p. 38, quoted in Alvarez, pp. 122-123.

[7]William Thomson, *A Trademan's Travels, in the United States and Canada, in the Years 1840, 41, & 42*, quoted in Alvarez, p. 124.

[8]Charles Klamkin, *Railroadiana*, Funk & Wagnalls, New York, 1976, pp. 1-2.

[9]Frank Munsey, *Railroad Man's Magazine*, October 1906, quoted in Klamkin, p. 1.

[10]"Reoriented Express," *Historic Preservation*, Vol. 43, No. 3, May-June 1991, National Trust for Historic Preservation, Washington, D. C., p. 42.

[11]Richard Snow and David Plowden, *The Iron Road: A Portrait of American Railroading*, Four Winds Press, New York, 1978, p. 16.

[12]Stanley Becker and Virginia B. Kunz, *The Collector's Book of Railroadiana*, Hawthorn Books, Inc., New York, 1976, p. 129.

[13]Lucius Beebe, "Purveyor to the West," *American Heritage*, February 1967, p. 30.

[14]Fredrika Bremer, *The Homes of the New World; Impressions of America*, Vol. I, Arthur Hall, Virtue, & Co., 1853, p. 346, quoted in Alvarez, p. 123.

[15]Brown, p. 144.

[16]*Ibid.*, p. 142.

[17]Henry A. Murray, *Lands of the Slave and the Free; Or, Cuba, the United States, and Canada*, Vol. I, John W. Parker and Son, London, 1855, p. 36, quoted in Alvarez, p. 124.

[18]Alvarez, p. 124.

[19]Brown, p. 227.

[20]Clifford, p. 166.

[21]*Ibid.*

[22]Frederick Marryat, *A Diary in America, with Remarks on its Institutions*, T. K. and P. G. Collins, 1840, pp. 9-10, quoted in Alvarez, pp. 124-125.

[23]Alistair Cooke, *Alistair Cooke's America*, Alfred A. Knopf, New York, 1973, p. 228.

[24]O. S. Nock, *Railways Then and Now*, Crown Publishers, Inc., New York, 1975, p. 41.

[25]Bill Bunce, *The Iron Horse Goes to War*, Association of American Railroads, Washington, D. C., 1960, p. 5.

[26]Brown, p. 74.

[27]*Ibid.*, p. 81.

[28]*Ibid.*, p. 145.

[29]*Ibid.*, p. 16.

[30]*Ibid.*, p. 67.

[31]Gen. Horace Porter, vice-president of the Pullman Palace-Car Company, 1893 quoted in Klamkin, p. 103.

[32]J. B. Jones, *A Rebel War Clerk's Diary at the Confederate States Capital*, edited by Howard Swiggett, Old Hickory Bookshop, New York, 1935, p. 361.

[33]*Appomattox Court House*, U. S. Department of the Interior, National Park Service, Washington, D. C., p. 6.

[34]Bunce, p. 16.

[35]Snow and Plowden, p. 24.

[36]Matthew Page Andrews, Editor, *The Women of the South in War Times*, The Norman Remington Company, Baltimore, 1920, pp. 62-63.

[37]Becker and Kunz, p. 129.

[38]Clifford, p. 169.

[39]*Ibid.*

[40]Becker and Kunz, p. 129.

[41]Brown, p. 234

[42]Arnold Palmer, *Movable Feasts*, Oxford University Press, New York, 1984, p. 80.

[43]*Ibid.*

[44]Nock, p. 91.

[45]Becker and Kunz, p. 90.

[46]*Ibid.*, p. 55.

[47]Klamkin, p. 108.

[48]Becker and Kunz, p. 130.

[49]Glenn, pp. 20-21.

[50]Jan McBride Carlton, *The Old-Fashioned Cookbook*, Holt, Rinehart and Winston, New York, 1975, p. 214.

[51]Becker and Kunz, pp. 130-131.

[52]*Ibid.*, p. 139.

[53]*Ibid.*, p. 130.

[54]Edith Bolling Wilson's description of France's presidential train in a letter, quoted by Frances W. Saunders, "Dearest Ones," *Virginia Cavalcade*, Autumn 1987, Virginia State Library, Richmond, VA, p. 55.

[55]"Reoriented Express," p. 42.

[56]Advertisement for the Great Rock Island Route, *Century Magazine*, August 1890, p. 77.

[57]Clifford, p. 166.

[58]*World Book Encyclopedia*, Vol. 15, Field Enterprises Educational Corp., Chicago, 1960, p. 106.

[59]Klamkin, p. 117.

[60]"Reoriented Express," p. 42.

[61]Klamkin, p. 108.

[62]Kelly, p. 44.

[63]*Ibid.*

[64]Beebe, p. 99.

[65]*Ibid.*, p. 47.

[66]Becker and Kunz, p. 130.

[67]Kelly, p. 46.

[68]*Ibid.*, p. 44.

[69]Beebe, p. 99.

[70]*Ibid.*, p. 28.

[71]Brown, p. 233.

[72]Beebe, p. 99.

[73]Kelly, p. 45.

[74]Will Rogers, quoted in Beebe, p. 99.

[75]Kelly, p. 46.

[76]Rushton, p. 12.

[77]Recipe courtesy Lois Ely, Ely's Grist Mill, Williamsport, OH.

[78]Ida Migliario, Editor, *The Household Searchlight*, *The Household Magazine*, Topeka, KS, p. 41, recipe contributed by Grace Viall Gray, Glen Ellyn, IL.

[79]Clifford, p. 166.

[80]Handwritten recipe, circa 1900, author unknown, author's private collection.

[81]Marvin Perry, *A History of the World*, Houghton Mifflin Co., Boston, 1985, p. 510.

[82]Recipe courtesy Epps Perrow, Hurt, VA.

[83]Recipe from the late Freida J. Hagberg, Chatham, VA.

[84]Brown, p. 144.

[85]*Ibid.*, p. 233.

[86]*Ibid.*, p. 142.

[87]*Ibid.*, p. 223.

[88]Recipe courtesy Mabel Combs, Chatham, VA.

[89]*Recipes for the Jewett Chafing Dish*, John C. Jewett Mfg. Co., Buffalo, NY, 1893, p. 23.

[90]*World Book Encyclopedia*, Vol. 10, p. 125.

[91]*Recipes for the Jewett Chafing Dish*, p. 45.

[92]Recipe courtesy Robert Martin, co-owner and chef of the Amalfi Harbour, Greensboro, NC.

[93]Klamkin, p. 130.

[94]*The Picayune's Creole Cook Book (Second Edition)*, The Picayune, New Orleans, 1901, reprinted by Dover, New York, 1971, p. 46.

[95]Recipe from Epps Perrow, Hurt, VA. She says, "[My] son Kirk [Perrow], III, 'invented' this one!"

[96]*Recipes for the Jewett Chafing Dish*, p. 46.

[97]*World Book Encyclopedia*, Vol. 15, p. 103.

[98]Recipe by Phyllis Gallant, *La Cuisine Acadienne*, compiled by Les Dames du Sanctuaire Mont-Carmel, provided by L'Association Touristique Evangéline, Wellington, Price Edward Island, p. 38.

[99]Recipe courtesy Mabel Combs, Chatham, VA.

[100]Migliario, p. 78.

[101]Becker and Kunz, p. 263.